South West Coast Path
Coastal Pub Walks
South Cornwall

AF066851

Part of the England Coast Path

First published 2024, reprinted in 2025 by:

Northern Eye Books Limited
Northern Eye Books, Tattenhall, Cheshire CH3 9PX
© Northern Eye Books Limited 2025

ISBN 978-1-914589-21-8

Text: *Fiona Barltrop*

Series editor: *Tony Bowerman*

Photographs: *Fiona Barltrop, Adobe Stock, Dreamstime, Shutterstock, Alamy*

Design: *Carl Rogers and Laura Hodgkinson*

Fiona Barltrop has asserted her rights under the Copyright, Designs and Patents Act, 1988 to be identified as the author of this work. All rights reserved

A CIP catalogue record for this book is available from the British Library.

Printed in the UK on woodland-friendly FSC stock

www.northerneyebooks.co.uk

 @northerneyebooks
@england_coast_path

 @northerneyeboo

 @northerneyebooks

For sales enquiries, please call 01928 723 744
tony@northerneyebooks.co.uk

Important Advice: The routes described in this book are undertaken at the reader's own risk. Walkers should take into account their level of fitness, wear suitable footwear and clothing, and carry food and water. It is also advisable to take the relevant OS map with you in case you get lost and leave the area covered by our maps.

Whilst every care has been taken to ensure the accuracy of the route directions, the publishers cannot accept responsibility for errors or omissions, or for changes in the details given. Nor can the publisher and copyright owners accept responsibility for any consequences arising from the use of this book.

If you find any inaccuracies in either the text or maps, please write or email us at the address above. Thank you.

This book contains mapping data licensed from the Ordnance Survey with the permission of the Controller of Her Majesty's Stationery Office. © Crown copyright 2025 All rights reserved. Licence number AC0000833184

Cover: *The Rashleigh Inn, Polkerris, (Walk 8) Alamy*

Contents

The South West Coast Path 4

Top 10 Walks: South Cornwall's coastal pubs .. 6

1 | **Old Success**, Sennen Cove 8

2 | **Logan Rock Inn**, Treen 14

3 | **Victoria Inn**, Perranuthnoe 20

4 | **Halzephron Inn**, Gunwalloe 26

5 | **Top House Inn**, Lizard 32

6 | **Plume of Feathers**, Portscatho 38

7 | **Ship Inn**, Portloe 44

8 | **Rashleigh Inn**, Polkerris 50

9 | **Old Ferry Inn**, Bodinnick 56

10 | **Devonport Inn**, Kingsand 60

Useful Information 64

South West Coast Path

Running for 630 miles from Minehead in Somerset, around the tip of Land's End and back to South Haven Point at the mouth of Poole Harbour in Dorset, the South West Coast Path is Britain's longest National Trail. Bordered by the Bristol and English channels and looking out to the open Atlantic, it encompasses some of England's most spectacular and wildest coastline, where the diversity of plant, animal and insect life can be stunning. The seas, coves and surrounding hinterland have been a dramatic setting for a gloriously rich history, and have inspired countless tales of romance, drama and intrigue.

This series of Top Ten Walks explores highlights along the way, showcasing the coast's natural beauty, wildlife and heritage and stimulating the imagination. Who knows, you may be inspired to come back to tackle the complete trail.

Visitors relaxing in the sun outside a Cornish coastal pub

Pubs along the South Cornwall Coast

Stretching for over 150 miles from Land's End in the far west to Plymouth Sound in the east, South Cornwall's Coast Path takes in a great variety of scenery, ranging from spectacular cliffs to sheltered estuaries, prominent headlands, beautiful beaches and little coves.

There are excellent hostelries to be found all the way along the coastline, either situated right on the coast or just inland.

As well as drinks and meals, a number also serve Cornish cream teas (jam first, cream on top – unlike Devon where it's the other way round!) Locally sourced produce, especially seafood, is used as much as possible.

"This was the land of my content"
— A.L. Rowse, poet, historian and 'voice of Cornwall'

TOP 10 Walks: South Cornwall's best coastal Pub Walks

EACH OF THE SELECTED CIRCULAR WALKS incorporates a stretch of the South West Coast Path, almost all starting and finishing close to the pub. The ten of them combined cover some of the finest sections of South Cornwall's coastline, one of great natural beauty and variety. With the pubs generally open all year and the walking good in all seasons, South Cornwall's coast is very much a year-round destination. These walks should whet your appetite to explore more of this wonderful coast, with other good pubs to be discovered, too.

Old Success Inn, Sennen Cove — page 8

Logan Rock Inn, Treen — page 14

Victoria Inn, Perranuthnoe — page 20

Ship Inn, Gunwalloe — page

Top House Inn, Lizard — page 32

Plume of Feathers, Portscatho — page 38

Ship Inn, Portloe — page 44

Rashleigh Inn, Polkerris — page 50

Old Ferry Inn, Bodinnick — page 56

Devonport Inn, Kingsand — page 60

The Old Success Inn's spacious seaside beer garden

walk 1

The Old Success
Sennen Cove

What to expect:
Steady climb at start, then easy walking along gently undulating granite cliff top Coast Path and field paths

Distance/time: 9 kilometres/5½ miles. Allow 3 hours.

Start: Beach car park, Sennen Cove (if full overflow car park at top of hill), or harbour car park at western end of cove

Grid ref: SW 355 263

Ordnance Survey map: Explorer 102 *Land's End*

The Pub: The Old Success Inn, Sennen Cove TR19 7DG | 01736 871232 | www.oldsuccess.co.uk

Walk outline: From the western end of the cove, the walk follows the Coast Path uphill onto the National Trust's Mayon Cliff, passing a former coastguard lookout, a superb viewpoint. Ahead is the Land's End headland to which the route continues along the top of the granite cliffs. The Coast Path keeps to the seaward side of the hotel and complex at Land's End with more spectacular cliff scenery to follow. At Mill Bay the walk turns inland and heads back across fields, rejoining the Coast Path at the lookout and thence back down to Sennen Cove.

Superbly situated looking out across Whitesand Bay and one of the most beautiful beaches in Cornwall, the highly popular Old Success is a 17th century former fisherman's inn.

Sunny beer garden

▶ The Old Success at a glance

Open: Daily from 11am to 11pm
Brewery/company: St Austell Brewery
Ales and wine: St Austell ales including Tribute and Proper Job. Extensive range of wines from around the world.
Food: Good choice of starters, pub classics and mains, including freshly caught seafood. Food served noon-2.30pm and 5-8pm
Accommodation: Twenty four rooms, including five dog-friendly ones, with beautiful views overlooking the beach
Outside: Beer garden and sun terrace.
Children & dogs: Both welcome.

The Walk

1. From the **beach car park**, return to the entrance and keep ahead past the **Old Success** on your left, following the pavement on the seaward side of the road, which provides wonderful views of **Whitesand Bay**. Pass the **lifeboat station** and beyond it the **Roundhouse and Capstan Gallery**. *This 19th century Grade II Listed Building was built to house a huge capstan wheel, which winched boats up and down the slip. The Capstan Gallery still features the old wheel, now used to display artwork.*

Carry on to the **harbour car park** at the end of the road. Turn left and keep ahead up the steps, following the **Coast Path** uphill. A steady climb brings you to the National Trust's **Mayon Cliff lookout** at **Pedn-Mên-du**.

Originally built as a Coastguard lookout, it was refurbished by the National Trust in 1998 and is open to the public during the summer. The views are spectacular, stretching north to Cape Cornwall and south to Land's End, taking in the Longships Lighthouse offshore.

2. Continuing along the well-waymarked Coast Path, soon a brief **detour** down to the right leads to a **cliff-edge viewpoint** above the inlet of **Castle Zawn** where the remains of **RMS Mulheim** can be spotted. A German cargo ship, built in Romania,

Sennen Cove harbour under a blazing summer sun

it was wrecked at Land's End in 2003. Just beyond, another right turn leads out to **Maen Cliff Castle**, an Iron Age promontory fort. Approaching **Land's End**, at a fork bear right out to the **First & Last House,** which sells refreshments and gifts.

The building stands on the most westerly point of mainland England, called Dr Syntax's Head. Dr Syntax appeared in William Combe's 1809 comic verse, ' The Tour of Dr Syntax in Search of the Picturesque', which satirised tourists seeking the 'perfect view'.

3. Continue along the surfaced path towards the **Land's End Hotel** (theme park behind), passing to the seaward side of it. You'll also pass the much-photographed **Land's End signpost**, with its distance markers. *On a clear day, the Scilly Isles, 28 miles away, can be seen.*

Keeping to the **main path** brings you to **Greeb Farm**, home to a collection of animals and craft shops. Just beyond it there's a fine view from above **Zawn Wells** of the sea stacks of Enys Dodnan (pierced by an arch) and the Armed Knight, with the Longships Lighthouse

Sennen Cove beach and Cape Cornwall

beyond. The Coast Path continues along the spectacular cliffs to beautiful **Mill Bay**, also known as **Nanjizal**.

4. At a **waymark post** (before reaching the footbridge below) turn left up steps and continue up the footpath to another waymark post. Keep ahead following the path as it bends left, then crosses a field, continuing through another to a hedge gap. The path angles left across this next field to the far hedge, bearing right alongside it to the hamlet of **Trevilley**. Keep ahead to the T-junction.

5. Turn right and immediately left at a **waymark post** across a stile. Continue through the **farmyard** and over a step stile into a field. Keep ahead along the right hand side of the field, across another stile and along the left side of the next field to a small gate in the corner. Go through this and past **cottages** to the road (**B3315**) at **Trevescan**. Turn left to the junction with the **A30**.

6. Cross to the drive signed for 'Treve Moor House', with a fingerpost signed for 'Sennen Cove ¾ mile'. Continue along this and when the drive bends left to the house, keep ahead along the narrow path by the waymark post. Cross a **footbridge** and the rough pasture beyond, keeping north through the following fields, aiming for the large white building — formerly Trinity House lighthouse keepers' cottages — in the distance. Cross a stile just before it and carry on beside a wall on the right. Join the drive and carry on past houses to where the road bends right. Keep ahead down a track signed 'Public Byway for 190 yards, Public Footpath to Sennen Cove ¼ mile'. Where the access road bends right, continue ahead past a gate down a track back to the **Mayon Cliff lookout**. Turn right to retrace initial steps back to the start. ♦

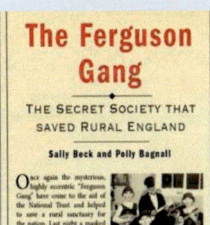

Mayon Cliff and Ferguson's Gang

The mysterious Ferguson's Gang, formed in 1927, were a group of well-educated young women, dedicated to preserving the countryside from the 'octopus' of urban development. They hid their identities behind colourful pseudonyms and raised huge sums for conservation. Their donations were delivered in strange ways and reported in the press. Thanks to a gift, the National Trust now protects 57 acres of land at Mayon and Trevescan Cliffs.

The flower-decked entrance to the 16th-century Logan Rock Inn at Treen

walk 2

The Logan Rock Inn
Treen

What to expect:
Granite cliff top Coast Path with some ups and downs; inland field paths and tracks

Distance/time: 8 kilometres/5 miles. Allow 3 hours.

Start: Treen village car park

Grid ref: SW 394 229

Ordnance Survey map: Explorer 102 *Land's End*

The Pub: The Logan Rock Inn, Treen, St Levan, Penzance TR19 6LG | 01736 810495 | **www.theloganrockinn.co.uk**

Walk outline: From Treen field and woodland paths lead down to the picturesque fishing cove of Penberth where the Coast Path is joined. Heading westwards it crosses the base of the Treryn Dinas headland with its Iron Age cliff castle and the Logan Rock. A seaward loop provides a fine view of beautiful Pednvounder beach, the Coast Path thereafter descending to Porthcurno bay. Climbing back uphill past the open-air Minack Theatre, the walk continues along the coast then heads inland via St Levan church to Porthcurno Telegraph Museum, and thence back to Treen.

Situated just a short walk inland from the Coast Path, the award-winning Logan Rock Inn is a 16th century traditional village pub.

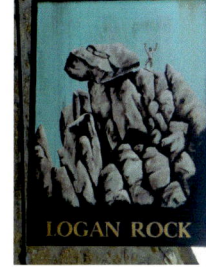

Painted inn sign

▶ Logan Rock Inn at a glance

Open: Daily from 11am to 11pm
Brewery/company: St Austell Brewery
Ales and wine: St Austell ales including Tribute, Proper Job and Logan Rock. Range of wines from around the world, plus Polgoon Cornish wines
Food: Choice of fish dishes including Logan Rock Fish Pie and Cornish Crab Macaroni, pub classics such as steak and ale pie, Cornish pasties, sandwiches and children's menu. Cornish cream teas. Food served noon-2.30pm and 5-8pm, noon-8pm at weekends; all day in summer.
Outside: Tables at the front and back.
Children & dogs: Both welcome.

The Walk

1. Exit the **car park** and turn immediately left down the grassy track/footpath alongside it. As the track bends right, keep ahead along the path, which turns left and then right. Cross a **stone stile** on the left and turn immediately right (signed for Penberth). Go through the gap in the hedge ahead and bear left across the field towards the corner of the hedge on the right. Continue beside the hedge on the right, cross another stone stile and carry on along the left hand edge of the next field. Cross a stile and follow the path down through the **woodland**, bearing right at the junction at the bottom. The path leads past a cottage to the small, picturesque fishing cove of **Penberth**, with its old capstan at the head of a granite cobbled slipway.

2. Turn right to follow the **Coast Path** uphill onto **Cribba Head**. Continuing westwards the Path crosses the base of the **Treryn Dinas headland** with its Iron Age promontory fort (or cliff castle), whose outer rampart the Path runs alongside. A **detour** out onto the headland is worthwhile. At its end is the **Logan Rock**, an example of a logan or rocking stone, said to weigh 80 tonnes.

In 1824 a group of British seamen dislodged the stone, knocking it off its perch. This upset the locals for whom it had become a tourist attraction and source of income, and the seamen were forced to restore it. The Logan Rock can still be rocked today, but much less easily than in the past.

Back on the Coast Path you'll come to a signed junction by a **granite stone**

Sky blue agapanthus frame seating at the famous Minack Theatre

bench. A **bridleway** turns inland to **Treen** —the route returns to this point later.

3. The Coast Path originally kept ahead here along the bridleway, but has now been re-routed to follow a more scenic option of a seaward loop. Fork left along the footpath and at the next fork take either the newer right hand path, signed as the Coast Path, or the lower left hand one (they join further on). Both provide wonderful views of the **Treryn Dinas headland**, with beautiful **Pednvounder beach** below backed by impressive cliffs. The latter passes a turning for a path which descends very steeply to the beach (note the warning sign and beware, too, the beach—which is popular with naturists—is covered at high tide). Rejoin the bridleway, turning left and then left again to **Percella Point**, where there's a **World War II pillbox**. *On the far side of Porthcurno beach below is the open-air Minack Theatre built into the cliff side.* Carry on downhill to the bottom of the hill.

4. The Coast Path continues round the back of the beach, but there are also steps up to it from the beach on the other side. A steep climb up steps is rewarded by

Caribbean colours from the cliffs at Porthcurno

superb views from the top, the **Minack Theatre** entrance just beyond.

The famous open-air theatre, created by Rowena Cade in the 1930s, is carved into the granite cliff and set in glorious sub-tropical gardens overlooking Porthcurno Bay. Performances at the Minack run from Easter to September, while the theatre and gardens are open to visitors all year.

Cross the car park to continue along the Coast Path, which leads down towards the next cove, **Porth Chapel**. Although the beach can be accessed, the Coast Path runs above it, then crosses a **footbridge** heading uphill and passing **St Levan's Well**. Carry on along the Coast Path to the next waymark post.

5. Turn sharp right and follow the footpath, soon along the left hand side of a field. Keep ahead where a path joins from the right, passing a house to the lane at **St Levan**. Cross to the track opposite, which leads into the **churchyard**.

6. Continue around the church to go up steps behind and keep ahead along the right hand side of the field. Go through a gate and across the next field to some houses, bearing left round them. Continue on a track heading northwards and at a fork keep right down to the road at Porthcurno.

Walk 2 – **The Logan Rock Inn,** Treen ♦ 19

7. Cross over and bear right along an entrance drive to the Telegraph Museum. Carry on past it down through the grounds to the car park. Follow the path from the bottom left corner towards the beach, taking the first left. Follow the bridleway uphill, rejoining the Coast Path and continue to point 3. Here turn left inland along the track back to Treen to complete the walk. ♦

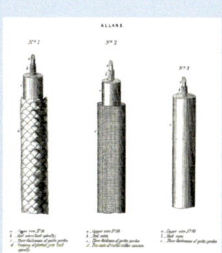

Porthcurno Telegraph Museum
Situated on the hillside above the car park and well worth a visit, this tells the story of Porthcurno's key role in the pioneering days of global communications. The small building above the beach is the Cable Hut. Built in 1929, this is where undersea telegraph cables came ashore from all around the world. It still has its original features and fittings and contains the largest collection of historic telegraph cables and termination boxes in the world.

Relaxing outside the Victoria Inn at the heart of Perranuthnoe

walk 3

Victoria Inn
Perranuthnoe

What to expect:
Fairly easy walking along gently undulating low cliffs and field paths

Distance/time: 8 kilometres/5 miles. Allow 3 hours.

Start: Perranuthnoe car park (charge)

Grid ref: SW 540 294

Ordnance Survey map: Explorer 102 *Land's End*

The Pub: Victoria Inn, Perranuthnoe, Penzance TR20 9NP | 01736 710309 | www.victoriainn-penzance.co.uk

Walk outline: The outward leg of this attractive circuit follows a charming stretch of the Coast Path south-eastwards around Mount's Bay, with views of its iconic focal point of St Michael's Mount. After rounding the promontory of Cudden Point, the Path reaches Prussia Cove, turning inland here for the return leg along field paths. The coastline, never far away, is still visible at intervals.

Set in the heart of the village just a few minutes walk from the Coast Path and beach, the Victoria Inn is renowned for its award-winning food, having been voted Dining Pub of the Year a number of times. Fine wines, local ales and a warm welcome await you, muddy booted walkers and wet dogs included.

Cornish ales

▶ The Victoria Inn at a glance

Open: Mon - Sat from noon-10pm (later in summer), Sun noon-8pm (10pm in summer)
Brewery/company: Free house
Ales and wine: Good local ales, Cornish cider, plus a choice of fine wines
Food: Excellent seasonal menus, locally sourced. Plus a choice of seafood dishes, vegetarian options and delicious desserts. Food served noon-2.30pm and 6-8.30pm (Mon-Sat), noon-4 (Sun)
Accommodation: Three en-suite rooms
Outside: South-facing terraced garden and further seating out the front
Children & dogs: Both welcome, dogs in bar and garden

St Michael's Mount tidal island, Mounts Bay from Perranuthnoe

The Walk .

1. Turn right out of the **car park** and walk back up the road. Take the first left just after the entrance to **Lynfield Craft Centre**, a former farmyard now converted into **art and craft shops**, which also houses the **Peppercorn Café**. Follow the lane uphill bending right, then keeping ahead up to a T-junction, the **church** opposite. *The church, which is dedicated to St Piran and St Michael, is of 12th century origin although subsequently rebuilt and restored; it is worth a look inside, especially to see the fine collection of kneelers.*

Turn left in front of the church and follow the lane to its end, continuing along the track until a **waymark post**, with an acorn symbol (for the South West Coast Path National Trail) on it, on the left.

2. Turn left down the enclosed path to the coast passing a **National Trust sign** on the way. At **Basore Point**, from where there is a fine view of St Michael's Mount, a **granite block-cum-bench** *has a dedication to John, Lord St Levan 1919 – 2013.*

The tidal island in Mount's Bay is linked to the mainland at Marazion by a causeway,

Walk 3 – **Victoria Inn**, Perranuthnoe ♦ 23

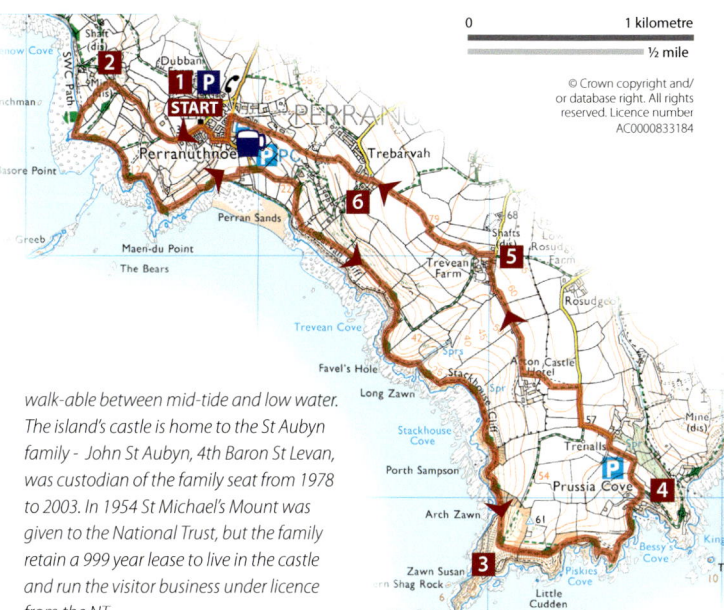

walk-able between mid-tide and low water. The island's castle is home to the St Aubyn family - John St Aubyn, 4th Baron St Levan, was custodian of the family seat from 1978 to 2003. In 1954 St Michael's Mount was given to the National Trust, but the family retain a 999 year lease to live in the castle and run the visitor business under licence from the NT.

Follow the **Coast Path** back to the road, the **car park** opposite; cross and continue along the access road to the right of it. Keep ahead where the road divides, soon on a path. Continue along the Coast Path, **Acton Castle** up on the hillside to the left coming into view. *The castellated mansion was built in the 18th century for John Stackhouse, a marine biologist, and named for his wife, Susanna née Acton. Several apartments are available as holiday lets.*

3. At **Cudden Point** ignore the path heading left inland and continue ahead around the coast via **Little Cudden** to **Piskies Cove**, one of a small group of coves that make up **Prussia Cove**. The Path continues above it to **Bessy's Cove**, passing a small **thatched fishermen's hut** on the left. At a fork bear left up steps and right along a track (**thatched cottage** to the left), keeping ahead

Sunrise over a calm sea at Prussia Cove

where another joins from the left to another fork/T-junction.

4. Turn left up the stony track (access road) to the lane and **car park** at the top. Continue along the lane which bends left and then right. One hundred and seventy metres further on, turn left over a stile (to the right of a gate) and walk along the left-hand side of the field, then bear diagonally right to another stile. Carry on along the left side of the next field, bending right in the corner to continue along the field edge path, which runs parallel to the access road on the left. Keep ahead in the next field and then the one after, watching for a stile on the left, a house in view ahead. Cross this and turn right along the road for a short distance.

5. On reaching the tarmac lane, turn left along a track signed 'Trevean Farm and Beare's Den Campsite'. When the track divides, left to the campsite, bear right and immediately left up **steps** to continue along a field-edge path. At the end of the field turn briefly right, then left over a stile and walk along the right-hand side of the next field. Go through a kissing gate and along the track bearing left at the lane and immediately right across a rough **parking area** past houses on the right.

6. Keep ahead along the field edge path, maintaining direction at the waymarked junction. The path leads back to **Perranunthoe**, passing in front of houses and joining an access road leading to the main village road, the **Victoria Inn** opposite. Turn left back down the **car park** to complete the walk. ♦

Prussia Cove

Prussia Cove—in fact a small collection of coves—is named after one of Cornwall's most famous smugglers, John Carter, the self-styled 'King of Prussia'. Together with his brother Harry, he ran a lucrative 18th century business, importing wine, spirits and tobacco from the French coast. The operations were run from the coves and caves around Prussia Cove. John Carter was also caretaker for Acton Castle and used the property as a hideout when the owner was away.

The historic Halzephron Inn at Gunwalloe

walk 4

Halzephron Inn
Gunwalloe

What to expect: *Easy walking along surfaced and unsurfaced tracks, modest gradients along grassy cliff-top Coast Path*

Distance/time: 12 kilometres/7¾ miles. Allow 4 hours

Start: Large free Fairground car park (opposite Boating Lake), Porthleven Road, Helston, TR13 0RA. Parking also available in Porthleven or at NT Penrose Hill car park

Grid ref: SW 654 270

Ordnance Survey map: Explorer 103 *The Lizard*

The Pub: Halzephron Inn, Gunwalloe, Helston TR12 7QB | 01326 240406 | www.halzephron-inn.co.uk

Walk outline: From Helston, the route follows the River Cober to The Loe, Cornwall's largest natural freshwater lake, which lies at the heart of the National Trust's Penrose estate. It is cut off from the sea by a large shingle bank, the Loe Bar, which the Coast Path crosses. The walk heads south along the coast from here to Gunwalloe, thereafter following the Coast Path northwards to finish at the fine harbour of popular Porthleven, with a short bus ride back to the start.

Situated just inland from the beach at Gunwalloe Fishing Cove on the Lizard Peninsula, the historic Halzephron Inn is full of character. It's an ideal refreshment stop on this scenically varied walk. There are more options at Porthleven, too, such as The Harbour Inn.

Chalkboard menu

▶ The Halzephron Inn at a glance

Open: Daily from Noon-10.30pm
Brewery/company: Free house
Ales and wine: Range of local ales, wide selection of wines from across the world and an extensive malt whisky collection.
Food: Excellent food, prepared using the freshest local produce. Seasonal menus. Book ahead. Food served noon-2.30pm (3pm on Sundays) and 6-9pm. Bar open all day, afternoon/cream teas also served
Accommodation: Two cosy cottage-style rooms
Outside: Picnic tables out the front, courtyard and beer garden
Children & dogs: Both welcome. 'Cornwall's most dog-friendly pub'

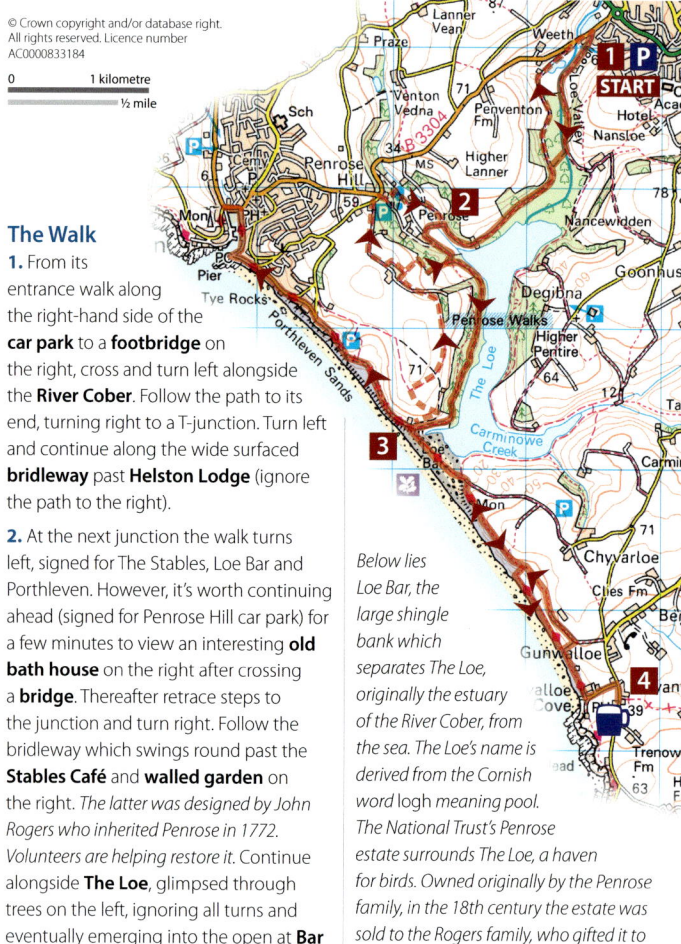

The Walk

1. From its entrance walk along the right-hand side of the **car park** to a **footbridge** on the right, cross and turn left alongside the **River Cober**. Follow the path to its end, turning right to a T-junction. Turn left and continue along the wide surfaced **bridleway** past **Helston Lodge** (ignore the path to the right).

2. At the next junction the walk turns left, signed for The Stables, Loe Bar and Porthleven. However, it's worth continuing ahead (signed for Penrose Hill car park) for a few minutes to view an interesting **old bath house** on the right after crossing a **bridge**. Thereafter retrace steps to the junction and turn right. Follow the bridleway which swings round past the **Stables Café** and **walled garden** on the right. *The latter was designed by John Rogers who inherited Penrose in 1772. Volunteers are helping restore it.* Continue alongside **The Loe**, glimpsed through trees on the left, ignoring all turns and eventually emerging into the open at **Bar Lodge**.

Below lies Loe Bar, the large shingle bank which separates The Loe, originally the estuary of the River Cober, from the sea. The Loe's name is derived from the Cornish word logh *meaning pool. The National Trust's Penrose estate surrounds The Loe, a haven for birds. Owned originally by the Penrose family, in the 18th century the estate was sold to the Rogers family, who gifted it to the National Trust in 1974. Penrose House*

Gunwalloe Fishing Cove beach on the South West Coast Path

(not open to the public) remains the family home.

3. Turn left and follow the **Coast Path** across **Loe Bar** continuing along the grassy cliffs past the **Anson memorial**. *This was erected in memory of the crew of HMS Anson, who were drowned when their ship was wrecked on Loe Bar in 1807. The tragedy prompted a Helston man, Henry Trengrouse, to invent a life-saving rocket apparatus, which subsequently saved thousands of lives.*

Carry on along the Coast Path to **Gunwalloe Fishing Cove**—there is a short signed official Coast Path diversion on a higher parallel path shortly before **Gunwalloe**. Note: *Swimming is dangerous both here and at Loe Bar*. Turn left up the lane to the T-junction, the **Halzephron Inn** across the road to the right.

4. Retrace your steps to the coast. A good spot for a swim is **Church Cove**, a further 2.5km/1½ miles south along a beautiful stretch of the Coast Path, but you can also swim at **Porthleven** at the end. Heading back north along the coast, continue on the higher

The pier and clocktower at Porthleven

parallel path at the end of the Coast Path diversion, re-joining the Coast Path a bit further on, thereafter re-crossing Loe Bar. Continuing north along the Coast Path, follow the new, well-signed route uphill from **Bar Lodge**, then along a higher-level path (the original one ran below) to **Porthleven**. At the end, the path descends steps to the road. Continue along the road to the splendid **harbour**, passing the **clock tower** near the **pier**, and round it to its north end where the bus stop is. There are regular buses between Porthleven and Helston via Penrose Hill.

Alternative options

Starting from the National Trust Penrose Hill car park (bus stop nearby) reduces the distance by a mile. From the car park follow the path near the information panel to a drive and turn right, then sharp left and right again continuing along the drive to waypoint 2.

To walk back to Helston—or the Penrose Hill car park—rather than finishing at Porthleven, head uphill from Bar Lodge, this time following signs for The Stables via Higher Penrose. Follow the gravel track to the junction (good views back over the coast and the Loe on the way). Keep ahead here along the bridleway signed for The Stables, Penrose Hill Car Park and Helston (the bridleway to the left leads to Porthleven). Continue along the grassy track to Higher Penrose. At the junction just before buildings turn left along the bridleway for Penrose Hill car park, otherwise, keep ahead along the footpath, signed for The Stables and Helston. The path descends through woodland to the valley, where the outward route is rejoined. Turn left and this time stay on the bridleway (Helston Drive) all the way back to car park to complete the walk. ♦

Helston

Described as the Gateway to the Lizard Peninsula, Helston is an historic market town. It is known for its impressive stone-sculpted buildings and 'kennels'—channels of water running alongside streets. The Museum of Cornish Life, where you can pick up a Heritage Trail leaflet, is well worth a visit. Helston is renowned for its ancient Furry Dance, part of the town's Flora Day festival held in May, which marks the passing of winter and arrival of spring.

The historic Top House Inn is Britain's southernmost pub

walk 5

The Top House Inn
Lizard

What to expect: *Grassy cliff top Coast Path with some ups and downs, inland track and lanes.*

Distance/time: 10 kilometres/6 miles. Allow 3 - 4 hours

Start: Lizard village green car park

Grid ref: SW 704 125

Ordnance Survey map: Explorer 103 *The Lizard*

The Pub: The Top House, Lizard, Helston TR12 7NQ | 01326 450098 | www.thetophouseinn.co.uk

Walk outline: Leaving Lizard village the walk heads east to Church Cove, where the Coast Path is joined for a circuit of the British mainland's most southerly point, Lizard Point. Heading southwards, the Lizard Lifeboat Station is passed, the Path continuing round Bass Point and Housel Bay to Lizard Point. From here, the route carries on round Lizard Head, then north to beautiful Kynance Cove. Steps are retraced to Caerthillian Cove, leaving the coast there to return inland to the village.

The welcoming 200-year old inn is the southernmost pub in the UK, within easy walking distance of Lizard Point. Friendly staff, quality food and a memorable place to stay.

Cream tea

▶ The Top House Inn at a glance

Open: Mon-Fri: noon-11pm, Sat & Sun: 10am-11pm
Brewery/company: St Austell Brewery
Ales and wine: Extensive drinks menu including fine St Austell ales and two guest beers; wide choice of wines, spirits and soft drinks
Food: All the pub favourites and extensive specials board. Fresh, locally sourced fish and seafood. Afternoon tea, including cakes
Accommodation: Eight beautiful 4* rooms, some with sea views
Outside: Tables out the front and in rear courtyard
Children & dogs: Both welcome. Dogs on wooden floor area (where some tables situated), not carpeted area, please

The Walk

1. From the **crossroads** at the southern tip of the **village green**, the bus stop opposite, cross the main road and follow the road signed for 'Church Cove'. Pass a turning on the right, and when the road forks, bear right, down past the village's **thatched cottages** and **St Wynwallow Church** to **Church Cove**. *This housed the original Lizard lifeboat from the first station at Polpeor Cove, when that was replaced with a new building and larger boat. The two were used together for 14 years until Church Cove station was closed in 1899. Today the former lifeboat house and other buildings are rented out as holiday accommodation.*

2. Before the parking area at the bottom of the access road, turn right onto the **Coast Path**. The path leads up onto the cliff top, shortly reaching the present-day **Lizard Lifeboat Station** at **Kilcobben Cove**.

The original station here was opened in 1961, replaced by a second station that opened in 2012. It is located at the foot of a high cliff, with a cliff railway above that carries the lifeboat crew down to the boathouse.

Continuing southwards, the cliff-top Coast Path leads to **Bass Point**, joining a track past **Bass Point House**, then forking left onto the Path that passes below the **National Coastwatch Institution lookout**.

The NCI lookout is one of 58 stations around the British coastline. These are manned by

Kynance Cove is owned and managed by The National Trust

over 2,600 volunteers, who keep a careful watch along the coast, reporting any incident or dangerous situation to the Coastguard. Visitors are normally welcome at the lookout, unless an incident is ongoing or training taking place. The red wall that the Coast Path passes below the lookout is an historic sea mark.

Behind the lookout is a white crenellated building, a disused Lloyds Signal Station—clearly visible looking back soon after the lookout. The station was operational from 1872, with ship to shore messages relayed using flags. It is now let as holiday accommodation.

3. Continuing along the Coast Path, you'll soon pass the former **Lizard Wireless Station**, in the care of the National Trust.

In 1900 the Italian inventor Guglieno Marconi undertook ground-breaking wireless experiments here on The Lizard. He also established a radio station on the cliff top near Poldhu Cove, along the west side of the Lizard Peninsula. One of the two cabins here near Lizard Point is now a holiday cottage.

The path passes below **Housel Bay Hotel** descending to cross a **footbridge** above **Housel Cove** (which can be

A gull's-eye view of the Lizard Point lighthouse and clifftop path

accessed by a flight of steep steps down to it). Then it's back uphill for an easy stretch to **Lizard Point**, passing the **Lizard Lighthouse** on the right. *Built in 1752, the lighthouse was automated in 1998. With money from the Heritage Lottery Fund, the engine room was later renovated to create a Heritage Centre, which opened in 2009. As well as learning about the workings of the lighthouse, visitors can climb to the top and enjoy the views.*

4. At **Lizard Point**, there's a **café** and **National Trust Wildlife Watchpoint**. The surfaced track carries on down past them to the disused **lifeboat house** at **Polpeor Cove** on the west side of the Point. The Coast Path continues up steps on the other side of the parking area, passing **Wavecrest Café** on the right. Steps lead down to a **footbridge** over a stream, the path continuing to **Lizard Head** and thereafter heading north along the grassy cliff-top. Further on, another flight of steps leads down to **Caerthillian Cove** and up the other side. A **bridleway** turns inland here at a waymark post, the return route to the village later.

5. The Coast Path carries on uphill passing above **Pentreath Beach**, soon reaching the cliff top overlooking **Kynance Cove**. This is one of Cornwall's beauty spots and duly popular (**café** and **public toilets** here). If you choose to go down to it, bear in mind the climb back up again afterwards. You can cross the beach if the tide is out; otherwise there's a **signed high tide route**.

6. Retrace steps to waypoint 5 and turn left at the waymark post up the path on the north side of the valley. Head gently uphill, and join a gravel track (access road) which leads past dwellings back to the car park to complete the walk. ♦

Lizard Point wildlife

At the Wildlife Watchpoint at Lizard Point you can learn more about the local wildlife. Grey seals are a common sight, along with dolphins, porpoises and other marine life. Birds here include choughs, a rare type of crow. A pair arrived at the Lizard in 2001, and were the first to breed in Cornwall in over 50 years. The chough (pronounced 'chuff') is distinguished by its red bill and legs.

Enjoying a sunny pint outside the Plume of Feathers, Portscatho

walk 6

Plume of Feathers
Portscatho

What to expect:
Gentle coastal path, wooded estuary and creek-side paths; track, private road and country lane

Distance/time: 9.5 kilometres/6 miles. Allow 3 hours. Longer option 15 kilometres/9½ miles. Allow 4½ hours

Start: Two National Trust car parks at Porth (or Gerrans car park for the longer walk option)

Grid ref: SW 867 329 or SW 873 350 (longer walk)

Ordnance Survey map: Explorer 105 *Falmouth & Mevagissey*

The Pub: The Plume of Feathers, The Square, Portscatho TR2 5HW | 01872 580321 | **www.plumeoffeathers-roseland.com**

Walk outline: St Anthony Head lies at the southernmost tip of the beautiful Roseland Peninsula, and is the focal point for this attractive walk, which encircles the promontory, open coast on one side, estuary and creek on the other. The walk begins at the National Trust's Porth car park, a short drive south of Portscatho, while the longer option starts from Gerrans village car park, a 5–10 minute walk from adjoining Portscatho.

Situated in the heart of the delightful village of Portscatho, just a stone's throw from the sea, the award-winning Plume of Feathers is duly popular, both with locals and visitors.

Hand-painted inn sign

▶ The Plume of Feathers at a glance

Open: Sun to Thurs 11am-11pm, Fri & Sat 11am-midnight
Brewery/company: St Austell Brewery
Ales and wine: St Austell ales including Tribute and Proper Job; also Timothy Taylor's Landlord and Cornish cider. Good selection of wines.
Food: Locally sourced food, including delicious seafood dishes. Vegetarian and gluten-free options. Also Sunday roasts, takeaways and children's menu. Food served daily from noon-8.30pm.
Accommodation: 5 bedrooms, all en-suite, including 2 dog-friendly ones
Outside: Tables and benches out the front
Children & dogs: Both welcome

The Walk

1. From **Porth**, cross the road from the **car park** and enter the **courtyard**. Go through the **roofed passage** past the **Thirstea Co tearoom**, and follow the path towards lovely **Towan Beach**, joining the **Coast Path** at the junction above it. Turn right, signed for St Anthony Head. The gentle cliff-top path leads round **Killigerran Head** and above **Porthbeor Beach**, passing another junction. Further on, the Path goes through a gate into the National Trust's **St Anthony Meadow**, soon reaching the **gun emplacements** and **toposcope** —a superb viewpoint— on **St Anthony Head**.

2. Continue along the **Coast Path** joining a drive that passes the converted **former officers' quarters** (now holiday cottages). Just before the car park turn left at a fingerpost and **information panel.** Take the left fork, down a few steps, then fork left again, leaving the Coast Path and following a narrower path signed for the battery observation post and bird hide. The path runs beside the **rampart**. From the **bird hide** return the same way, turning left back onto the Coast Path. Continue down the surfaced path to another junction. The Coast Path turns sharp right here, but continue ahead for a short distance to view the **lighthouse** (now holiday accommodation), built in 1835. Return to the Coast Path keeping ahead, soon passing a **small building**

Walk 6 – **Plume of Feathers**, Portscatho

A sub-tropical garden surrounds the ancient church of St Just, in Roseland

on the left, a former paraffin store for the lighthouse. Just after a gate, a signposted junction is reached.

3. Bear left to continue on the Coast Path which descends to cross the top of a **dam**, passing above the adjoining **Molunan beaches**. The Path gently rises, soon turning right up a flight of steps and rounding **Carricknath Point** - St Mawes Castle, one of Henry VIII's artillery forts, can be seen across the water. Continuing above the shore, the view of yachts anchored in St Mawes Harbour is a picturesque sight. Before reaching the trees around **Amsterdam Point**, the Path angles right up the grassy slope, goes through a gate at the top and back down the other side.

4. At the bottom bear right along a track. When it divides keep left, and likewise at the next fork, then left down steps to the **church**. *The beautiful 12th/13th century Church of St Anthony in Roseland, with its fine Norman doorway, is in the care of the Churches Conservation Trust.* Walk through the **churchyard** past the **medieval coffin**. At the lane turn left, passing the entrance to splendid **Place House**

St Anthony Head sits at the southernmost tip of the Roseland Peninsula

fronted by its large lawn on the left. *Built in 1840, it is the Spry family home.*

5. Just before the **slipway** at the end of the lane, turn right to continue along the path, passing steps that lead down to the pontoon **ferry point** for St Mawes. Two ferries are required to cross between Place and Falmouth (via St Mawes)—where the Coast Path continues. However, this walk carries on along the woodland path beside the **Percuil River** to **North-hill Point**, and then beside **Porth Creek**. Ignore the two junctions (paths signed for 'Bohortha') along the way. Near the end the path runs along the bottom of a field. Bear left at the signposted junction along a track and right at the next junction back to **Porth car park**.

Longer option

Starting from **Gerrans car park**, turn left along the lane for 180 metres, then left along an enclosed footpath signed for Portscatho. Go through a gate, cross a track and follow the path diagonally across the field to a fork at the corner. Bear right heading gently down beside the hedge on the right to reach a track. Cross it diagonally left, go through a gap in the hedge and continue on the footpath down the left side of the field to the **Coast Path**. Turn right and follow it to **Towan Beach**, joining the main walk there.

For the return from **Porth**, turn left up the lane from the car park and very soon fork right onto a track/bridleway. Further on, it continues as a grassy track leading to **Rosteague**. Carry on along the private access road, which joins the lane leading back to the car park to complete the walk. ♦

St Anthony Head

Overlooking the mouth of the estuary of the River Fal, known as Carrick Roads—the third largest natural harbour in the world—the headland has long been of strategic importance and duly fortified. Most of what survives today dates from the late 19th/early 20th century and is now in the care of the National Trust, which has restored the gun battery and its magazine. On the headland opposite is Pendennis Castle, an artillery fort built by Henry VIII also to defend the waterway.

The Ship Inn is a traditional Cornish village pub

walk 7

The Ship Inn
Portloe

What to expect:
Coast Path, strenuous ups and downs; field paths, country lanes; extension along sandy beach

Distance/time: 11.5 kilometres/7 miles. Allow 3½ hours

Start: Portloe village car park TR2 5RE

Grid ref: SW 938 396

Ordnance Survey map: Explorer 105 *Falmouth & Mevagissey*

The Pub: The Ship Inn, Portloe | 01872 228954 | www.shipinnportloe.com

Walk outline: Starting from Portloe, one of Cornwall's prettiest villages, situated on the lovely Roseland Peninsula, the walk follows the Coast Path via Nare Head to Carne Beach. From here the route heads inland taking in Carne Beacon—one of the largest Bronze Age barrows in England—and the charming village of Veryan, known for its thatched roundhouse cottages. The final leg heads east via the hamlet of Trewatha and thence back down to Portloe.

Within sight of the sea, the traditional Ship Inn features a single cosy bar and a sunny split-level beer garden over the road opposite the pub.

Indoor pub sign

▶ The Ship Inn at a glance

Open: Every day except Tuesday (open every day in summer): noon-10pm. Food 12-3pm, 5-9pm (summer), 12-2pm, 5-8pm(winter)
Brewery/company: St Austells Brewery
Ales and wine: Real ales include St Austell Tribute and Proper Job, guest ale, and lagers; good selection of wines
Food: Home cooked, locally sourced traditional pub food. Food served 12-3pm, 5-9pm
Accommodation: One family room and one en-suite double (B&B)
Outside: Attractive beer garden
Children & dogs: Both welcome

During the Second World War both Nare Head and its twin site, Nare Point, further down the coast south of Falmouth Bay, were used as decoy sites to protect the port of Falmouth. Special effects were used to simulate lights from the docks and railway to lure enemy bombers away from their intended target.

In 1962 an underground bunker was built for use in the Cold War, when a nuclear attack was considered a threat. It was intended to accommodate three officers from the Royal Observer Corps, who could live there for up to three weeks, monitoring radioactive fallout following a nuclear attack.

The Walk

1. Turn left out of the **car park** down the lane, then left down towards the **harbour**, the **Lugger Hotel** on the left, and right at the **Coast Path** fingerpost. Head up past the **public toilets**, continuing round **Jacka Point**. The Coast Path takes you round **Manare Point** and thereafter **Blouth Point** and on towards **Nare Head**.

2. On **Rosen Cliff** you'll come across the grassed-over command bunker of a Second World War decoy site and ventilator turrets of a Royal Observer Corps nuclear bunker.

3. Before rounding the headland, turn

Portloe is a busy fishing village

left to follow the path that leads out to its tip, a superb viewpoint. Offshore is **Gull Rock**, a breeding ground for seabirds. Rejoin the main path which heads northwards and descends to a valley (**Tregagle's Hole**) passing the remains of an **old fisherman's cottag**e and crossing a **footbridge**.

The stone and cob cottage belonged to a 19th century fisherman called Mallett, who lived here during the week, returning to his wife in Veryan at weekends. In due course he emigrated to Australia without her.

The route continues up the other side and thereafter down to a road. Turn left down to **Carne Beach**. If the tide is out you could extend the walk along lovely **Carne** and **Pendower** beaches, returning along the Coast Path. *Overlooking the two is the Nare country house hotel, Cornwall's highest rated hotel.*

4. Turn right inland to the **National Trust car park** and walk through it to its far right corner. Go through a kissing gate and continue along the grassy valley to a fingerpost and **footbridge** on the left. Fork right here and head diagonally uphill to the gap in the bushes, passing

The pretty coastal village of Portloe on the Roseland Peninsula

Veryan Castle, an oval area surrounded by ramparts, possibly an Iron Age homestead. Go through the kissing gate and follow the right-hand side of the field to a lane. Turn right for a short distance, then fork left across two stiles and through the field to **Carne Beacon** —there are steps to the top.

5. Return the same way to the lane, and immediately take the other footpath forking right along the right-hand side of the field to another road. Turn right to **Veryan** and keep ahead through the village past the **two roundhouses** and **New Inn** to the **war memorial** and **church** on the right.

There are five roundhouse cottages in the village, each with a thatched conical roof and topped by a cross. Dating to the 19th century, they were built for the Reverend Jeremiah Trist, the local vicar. Legend has it they were constructed without corners so the Devil would be unable to hide in them.

The church of St Symphorian is a mixture of Norman, medieval and 19th century work. In the churchyard can be found what is reputed to be the longest marked grave in Britain.

6. Just beyond fork right along a surfaced path signed to 'Portloe via Trewetha'. Keep right passing the green, then leave the path on the right through a gap in the trees crossing a footbridge and stile into a field. Head up by trees on the right, then angle left uphill to the tree line at the top and go through a gate. Continue through the next field to join a track leading to a lane. Turn left then right via Trewetha, continuing along the footpath on the right-hand side of the field, then climb a step stile over the wall on the right. Descend the field to houses and a lane and turn left back to the car park to complete the walk. ♦

Nare Head

Enclosing Gerrans Bay to the east is the prominent headland of Nare Head. It is not only a superb viewpoint but also has a fascinating history as both a WW2 decoy site and later as the location of an atomic early warning bunker. Two long fine sandy beaches stretch out along Gerrans Bay to the west, while to the east of the headland the coastline is one of rugged cliffs and inaccessible coves.

The Rashleigh Inn sits right on the beach at Polkerris

walk 8

Rashleigh Inn
Polkerris

What to expect:
Inland paths and country lanes; coast path along field edges and cliff tops; lots of ups and downs

Distance/time: 10.5 kilometres/6½ miles. Allow 3½ hours

Start: Polkerris village car park (charge); alternatively Tregaminion overflow field car park above Polkerris, near Point 2

Grid ref: SX 094 523

Ordnance Survey map: Explorer 107 *St Austell & Liskeard*

The Pub: The Rashleigh Inn, Polkerris, Par PL24 2TL | 01726 814685 | www.therashleighinn.co.uk

Walk outline: From the attractive sandy cove at Polkerris, on the western side of the Gribbin promontory, the walk follows the Coast Path uphill, leaving it to continue inland along part of the Saints' Way, a waymarked trail that crosses Cornwall from the north to south coast. This leads to the other side of the promontory at the entrance to Fowey harbour. Here the Coast Path is rejoined, passing St Catherine's Castle, and thence back to Polkerris via Gribbin Head, with its tower.

The historic Rashleigh Inn is positioned right beside the beach, with lovely views across the bay and beautiful sunsets. In the past Polkerris was important for its pilchard fishing industry.

Beach terrace

▶ The Rashleigh Inn at a glance

Open: Sun-Thurs 11am-10pm, Fri & Sat 11am-11pm
Brewery/company: Free house
Ales and wine: Choice of locally produced traditional cask ales and craft ales, which change regularly. Wide selection of wines.
Food: Fresh, local, home-cooked food every day. Dishes include vegetarian and vegan options. Roasts on Sundays. Food served noon to 8pm.
Outside: Terrace above the beach with views of cove, protected by its curving harbour wall, and St Austell Bay
Children & dogs: Both very welcome.

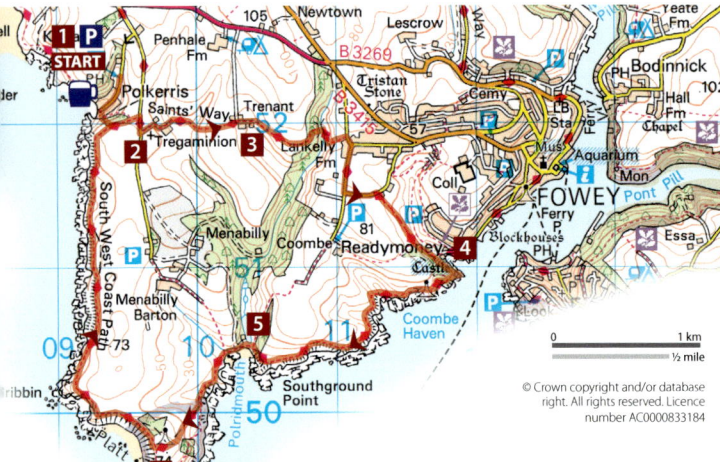

© Crown copyright and/or database right. All rights reserved. Licence number AC0000833184

The Walk

1. Turn right out of the **car park** down the lane its end, passing between the old lifeboat station, now **Sam's On the Beach Restaurant**, and the **Rashleigh Inn** to reach the beach. Turn immediately left in front of Sam's and up a ramp, then right up **steps** and continue up the zigzag **Coast Path** through woods to the top. (If starting from the Tregamion field car park, turn right out of it along the lane to join the route just after point 2.)

2. Leave the Coast Path, which turns right, and keep ahead along the path across the field to a metal gate and lane. Turn right for 120 metres, then left just before the **church**, a fingerpost on the right signed **The Saints' Way**, a section of which the walk now follows. *The Saints' Way, which is well signed with Celtic cross waymarks, crosses mid Cornwall from Padstow on the north coast to Fowey on the south, a distance of about 30 miles.* Head down the access road, turning right to follow the track signed for 'Fowey', then left by the **farm buildings**. Go through a gate and follow the path round the bottom right of the field, cross a **footbridge** and climb a long flight of **steps**. The path leads to a lane at **Trenant**.

3. Go straight across to continue along the enclosed path, which crosses a **stone stile** and descends through **woodland**, going under a **bridge** and across a **stream**.

Aerial view of St Catherine's Castle, near Fowey

Continue uphill to reach a lane and turn right. Keep ahead at the junction along **Prickly Post Lane** and take the next left. Turn right after 230 metres to continue down the **Saints Way**, keeping ahead at a junction down through the wood to the next, where the Coast Path is joined. The route carries on ahead along it, but to visit **Readymoney Cove**—a worthwhile detour—turn left downhill for a short distance. *The sheltered sandy beach is a popular swimming spot. There are also* **toilets** *and a* **café/shop** *here. The building with the turrets used to be a limekiln.* Retrace steps to the junction.

4. Continuing on the Coast Path ignore a right turn and another turning back down to the left, then fork left to head out to **St Catherine's Point** and **Castle**, from where there are superb views of Fowey harbour. *On the opposite side of the harbour entrance is the village of Polruan.*

St Catherine's Castle, cared for by English Heritage (free, open all year), is a small artillery fort built in the 1530s by Henry VIII to protect Fowey harbour. In the mid 19th century during the Crimean War, a two-gun battery was added below it. The battery was used again during the Second World War.

Cottage, lake and beach at Polridmouth Bay, near Fowey

Return to the main path and turn left to continue on the Coast Path, passing a **shelter** with some **information panels** up on the right. The Path turns left and goes through a gate out onto the open grassland of **Alldays Fields** (presented to the people of Fowey in 1951). It continues down to **Coombe Haven**, then uphill again and around the coastline, descending steps to the attractive cove and beach at **Polridmouth** (pronounced Pridmouth).

The building (a holiday let) and private lake belong to the historic Menabilly estate. The mansion house, situated in woodland inland from here, has been home to the Rashleigh family from the 16th century until the present day. Daphne du Maurier lived there for many years, leasing it from the family. Menabilly was the inspiration for Manderley in her novel Rebecca. *During the Second World War, Polridmouth was used as a decoy site, lights placed round the lake to lure enemy bombers away from Fowey harbour.*

5. Cross the **stream** and walk round the cove past the adjoining beach, then over the **boardwalk** and down the grass. Go through the gate and climb the steps, continuing up the field to the **Gribbin daymark**.

6. After rounding the headland the Coast Path runs high above a cove called **The**

Platt, then heads northwards along the western flank of the **Gribbin peninsula**, with fine views across St Austell Bay. *Par Docks, situated on the far side, was used in the past for the export of china clay, an important industry in this part of Cornwall.*

The conical mounds formed by the waste have been dubbed the Cornish Alps. On reaching point 2, retrace initial steps back down to **Polkerris** to complete the walk. ♦

Gribbin Head
Situated atop the headland, which separates St Austell Bay from the Fowey estuary, is the Gribbin Tower, a prominent landmark from afar. This 84ft high red and white striped daymark, constructed in Greco-Gothic style, was built in 1832 by Trinity House as a navigation aid. You can climb to the top of it on some Sundays in summer. The tower and headland, which supports a variety of wildlife, are in the care of the National Trust.

The Old Ferry Inn is a stone's-throw from the Fowey-Bodinnick ferry

walk 9

The Old Ferry Inn
Bodinnick

What to expect: *Woodland paths with ups and downs, steep climb up lane at start, town streets*

Distance/time: 6.5 kilometres/4 miles. Allow 3 hours

Start: Bodinnick slipway. Small car park 300m up main road on right-hand side; alternatively Caffa Mill car park on Fowey side of river next to ferry slipway or Quay car park, Polruan

Grid ref: SX 129 522

Ordnance Survey map: Explorer 107 *St Austell & Liskeard*

The Pub: The Old Ferry Inn, Bodinnick, Fowey PL23 1LX | 01726 870237 | www.theoldferryinn.co.uk

Walk outline: Known as the Hall Walk, this popular circuit of Fowey Harbour and its eastern arm, Pont Pill, involves two ferry crossings. It can be started from Fowey, Bodinnick or Polruan, all of which have car parks. The ferry between Fowey and Bodinnick takes cars and foot passengers, the other between Fowey and Polruan is pedestrians only. Both add to the pleasure of the walk, with some beautiful views along the way.

Situated on the hillside with stunning views over the harbour, the 17th century Old Ferry Inn has long provided rest and refreshment for travellers using the Bodinnick ferry, an important river crossing. The Inn has its own distillery. Pubs in Fowey and Polruan, too.

Terrace view

▶ The Old Ferry Inn at a glance

Open: 10am-midnight
Brewery/company: Free house
Ales and wine: Traditional Cornish and craft ales; quality wine list; own distillery, producing own 'Yards' branded spirits
Food: Locally sourced ingredients with menus changing regularly, Sunday roasts, Cornish cream teas. Food served noon-3pm, 6-9pm
Accommodation: 11 rooms, 8 with river views. Terrace hot tub for staying guests. One of the *Sunday Times* 100 best places to stay in Britain
Outside: Terraces with sunny south-west facing views of the harbour
Children & dogs: Both welcome, dogs in the bar area

The Walk

1. From the **slipway** walk straight up the steep lane ahead of you, passing the **Inn** on your left. Just after it on the right is charming little **St John's Church**, *which was converted in 1948 from a stable.* Continue uphill for another 70 metres and turn right along a path between houses, signed **Hall Walk**, soon reaching a **memorial stone** and **bench**—one of a number along the route, positioned at viewpoints. Keep ahead to the next monument, just past a **shelter** on the left (do read the plaque in it). This **'Q' memorial**, situated at a splendid viewpoint above **Penleath Point**, *commemorates Sir Arthur Quiller-Couch, novelist and scholar, who was known as 'Q'. He lived in Fowey from 1891 until his death in 1944.*

2. Now heading eastwards, the high-level path continues along the northern side of **Pont Pill**. The path leaves the woodland through a gate to follow the field edge for a short distance, then re-enters the trees at another gate and path junction. At the next junction, turn sharp right, as signed, and continue down to the small hamlet of **Pont**. This was once a busy quay where barges would unload their cargo. **Pont Pill Farmhouse** (once a pub), **Pont Creek Cottage** and **Mohun** are National Trust holiday cottages.

3. Cross the **footbridge** and follow the path up past the cottages and an old **lime kiln** on your right. At the junction turn right, signed for Polruan. The path heads uphill to go through a gate and then along the top of a field, further on continuing through **woodland**. Keep following the signs for Polruan

Cars and foot passengers board the ferry below the Old Ferry Inn at Bodinnick

at junctions. Cross an access road to continue along the path which leads down to **Polruan**, descending **steps** and turning left along **East Street** to the **quay**. Continue along **West Street** to its end to visit the **Blockhouse**.

4. Take the **ferry** across to **Fowey** which in the daytime in summer lands you at **Whitehouse Pier**, and in winter the **Town Quay**. From both landing points turn right, following the **Esplanade** from the former to the **Town Quay**, continuing along **Fore Street** to **Caffa Mill car park** and the **ferry** for **Bodinnick**. *The large house on the water's edge in view as you approach Bodinnick is Ferryside, which was bought by the du Maurier family in 1926. It was here that Daphne du Maurier wrote her first novel,* The Loving Spirit.

Fowey and Polruan
Fowey (pronounced 'Foy' to rhyme with joy) is a lovely place with much to see and plenty of historic interest. During the summer months the harbour is always busy with yachts, fishing boats and ferries. Picturesque Polruan is also worth exploring. As well as the 15th century blockhouse, which with its twin across the water guarded the harbour entrance, there are superb views from the top of the hill, reached via a climb up Battery Lane, following the Coast Path signs.

The stylish Devonport Inn at Kingsand

walk 10

The Devonport Inn
Kingsand

What to expect: *Coast Path, woodland, open, exposed cliffs; village streets, quiet country lanes and field paths*

Distance/time: 10.5 kilometres/6½ miles. Allow 3½ - 4 hours

Start: Kingsand Car Park, Fore Street

Grid ref: SX 433 505

Ordnance Survey map: Explorer 108 *Lower Tamar Valley & Plymouth*

The Pub: The Devonport Inn, The Cleave, Kingsand, Torpoint PL10 1NF | 01752 822869 | www.devonportinn.com

Walk outline: Situated in the south-east of the county, the Rame Peninsula is often referred to as Cornwall's Forgotten Corner, but it is well worth visiting. The walk round the peninsula makes an excellent circuit. From Kingsand the route heads south through Cawsand, then follows the wooded coastline out to Penlee Point. It continues along open cliffs to wonderful Rame Head and its medieval chapel atop the headland, a superb viewpoint. From here the walk heads northwards to Whitsand Bay, then back inland across the the headland.

Perched above the beach with views across Cawsand Bay, the pub is known for its welcoming atmosphere, great service and excellent food.

Seafront pub seats

▶ The Devonport Inn at a glance

Open: 11am-11pm
Brewery/company: Free house
Ales and wine: Local real ales, Cornish ciders and an extensive wine list. Also cocktails and alcohol-free drinks.
Food: Good choice of starters, tasty main courses (local seafood a speciality) and tempting desserts. Daily specials. Food served 12-2.30pm (3pm on Sundays) and 6-9pm. Hot Cornish pasties served all day 11am-9pm; Cornish Cream teas from 11am-5.30pm.
Outside: Tables out the front with views across the bay
Children & dogs: Both very welcome, the latter on leads

The Walk

1. Turn right out of the **car park** and right again along **Garrett Street** (or keep ahead past the **Clock Tower** for the **Devonport Inn**, then retrace steps). Follow Garrett Street to **Cawsand** and its **square** and thereafter turn left into **Pier Lane,** signed Coast Path. The lane/track leads through **woodland** to the fine **viewpoint** of Penlee Point, where you emerge from the trees, now on a surfaced drive. As it bends right, descend some steps on the left and continue down the path to the 19th century **grotto** *built for visit of Princess (later Queen) Adelaide*. Retrace steps to the top. *The headland's former* **Penlee Battery,** *now a nature reserve, was part of the defence of Plymouth Sound.*

2. Continue along the Coast Path, initially on a drive and then path. At a path junction/stile, a brief **detour** to visit **Rame Church** is recommended. Cross the stile on the right and follow the field edge path up to the lane and turn left. Opposite the **Old Rectory** (*outside which you may find bottles of home-made apple juice for sale*) fork left along the track to **St Germanus Church**, which dates to the 13th century.

3. Retrace steps to the **Coast Path**, turning right to continue to **Rame Head**, grazed by ponies. Divert from the Coast Path up the path/steps to the 14th century **St Michael's Chapel** atop the headland, which affords fine views.

4. Return to the Coast Path and carry on northwards, in due course bearing left at a waymark post and descending steps to cross a drive leading down to **Polhawn Fort**. Continue down steps opposite, and then along a cliff side path, soon reaching a small gate on the left by a **Whitsand**

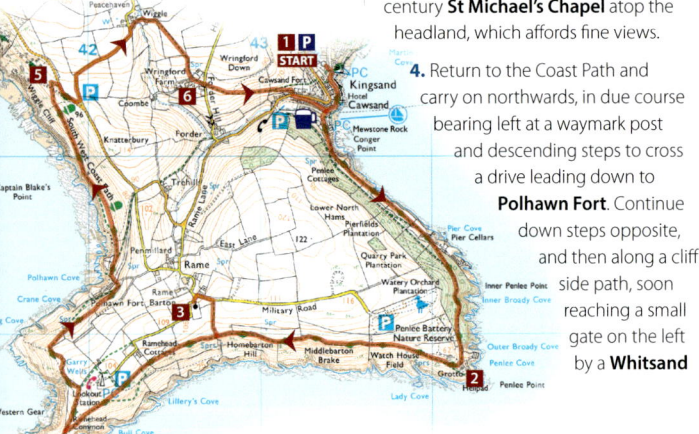

© Crown copyright and/or database right. All rights reserved. Licence number 100047867

The clock tower at Kingsand is a local landmark

Bay information panel. Further on the Coast Path ascends to reach a track just below the road.

5. Leaving the Coast Path, bear right up the track to the road. Cross diagonally right to the lane opposite and bear left at the next junction. Follow the lane for about 500 metres to **Wiggle**, then fork right along a signed path, which leads to an open field. Head diagonally down it, and thence down to a drive at **Wringford** bearing left to a lane.

6. Cross the road and continue down the field path to a stile and kissing gate on the left. Keep ahead downhill to the road. Cross and carry on down **St Andrews Street**, then left along **Garrett Street** back to **Kingsand**.

Rame Head

The Rame Peninsula is the smallest of the 12 separate geographical areas that make up the Cornwall National Landscape. The area is located on the western side of Plymouth Sound and takes in Mount Edgcumbe Country Park, Penlee Point and Rame Head itself. Sheltered by the headland are the adjoining seaside villages of Kingsand and Cawsand with a long history of both fishing and smuggling.

Useful Information

South West Coast Path Association
A charity that champions the South West Coast Path, as well as helping fund path repairs and improvements. **www.southwestcoastpath.org.uk** | 01752 896237

Visit Cornwall
The county's official tourism website covers everything needed to plan and book a holiday or short break in South Cornwall **www.visitcornwall.com**

Cornwall National Landscape
The Cornwall National Landscape is Cornwall's Protected Landscape with the same status and protection as a National Park. **https://cornwall-landscape.org**

Tourist Information Centres
The TICs provide free information and advice on everything from accommodation and transport to what's on and walking advice.

Penzance	01736 335530
Falmouth	01326 741194
Truro	01872 274555
Mevagissey	01726 842200
Fowey	01726 833616
Looe	01503 262255

South Cornwall Breweries and Pubs
There are over two dozen breweries in Cornwall producing award-winning real ales and craft beers, plus some twenty or so real cider makers. For details of the encouragingly high number of real ale pubs in Cornwall, see the local CAMRA website, or buy a copy of their excellent annual *Good Beer Guide*, its 50th anniversary edition published in 2023. Visitors can also sample a mouth-watering range of local real ales and ciders at the many beer festivals held throughout the year. See: **www.cornwall.camra.org.uk.**

Rail travel
Mainline railway stations are located at Penzance, Truro, St Austell and Plymouth/ Saltash with others serving the coast at Falmouth and Looe. See: **www.thetrainline. com** or **www.nationalrail.co.uk** (03457 484950)

Bus travel
Many places along the South Cornwall coast are served by bus. See **www. transportforcornwall.co.uk** or **www.travelinesw.com** (0871 200 2233)